4

5

9

10

11

14

15

19

20

Welcome to *Cross Stitch for the Heart* – a book filled with patterns celebrating all aspects of love, kindness, compassion and connection.

Life and love are precious, and the last two years have made me realize this more acutely than ever before. I think it's safe to say that living during a pandemic has made us all reassess what we value in our own lives. We've all missed our loved ones through lockdowns, and many have suffered losses too. We've seen a lot of kindness during this time as well: communities coming together, strangers helping each other, the tireless work of healthcare professionals and key workers to keep things going despite all the challenges and risks they face every day. It's highlighted the importance of human connection and how it benefits us all in multiple ways.

These 20 patterns celebrate love and connection in different ways. Like all of my work, they are designed to be uplifting to view as well as enjoyable to stitch.

CROSS STITCH FOR THE Heart

20 DESIGNS to Love

DAVID & CHARLES

www.davidandcharles.com

Contents

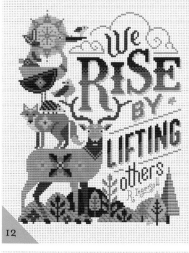

Tools and Materials

Fabric

When it comes to fabric there are so many options, but Aida is a great choice. The pre-woven holes make stitching a breeze. I'm all about enjoyment when it comes to stitching and, as much as I appreciate the neatness of Jobelan or Hardanger, I find Aida much easier to work with.

Throughout this book I have recommended specific fabrics to use for each piece. These are chosen to work best with the colours but, of course, substitutions can always be made to suit your own style and material choices. Here's a simple breakdown of the fabric types you might want to consider:

- Aida is an open, evenweave, cotton fabric. It has a natural mesh that helps guide the stitcher, and enough stiffness that, for smaller projects at least, an embroidery hoop isn't always required.

- Fiddler's cloth is similar to Aida but is slightly irregular, producing a more rustic, aged look, which is good if you want something a little less perfect.

- Hardanger is made of 100% cotton at 22-count weave. Usually used for 'Hardanger embroidery', it also works for cross stitch and gives a fine finish. It's trickier to work with than Aida because of its denser weave but the results can be well worth it.

Sustainability

Cotton, although a natural fabric, does use a lot of water and pesticides to produce, and contributes to environmental pollution when not farmed in an organic way. I always try to waste as little of it as possible when working with it.

Organic cotton is considerably better for the environment but is not widely available for cross stitching at this present moment (though hopefully it will be in the future).

Linen, when farmed correctly, has a much lower carbon footprint than cotton so makes an excellent choice for those wanting to be a little bit more conscious about the impact of their materials.

- Linen has a crisp feel and a finer weave than Aida, and is usually stitched over two threads of the fabric. It offers a more traditional look. Working with linen can also be a challenge, so you might want to consider 'linen Aida', which combines the qualities of both.

- Jobelan is a soft fabric with a slight sheen. It is also stitched over two threads, but is more resistant to wrinkles compared to linen. It's easy to wash, so is ideal for larger projects for the home, such as tablecloths and pillows.

Thread

Thread is the paint of the stitching world and offers endless creative possibilities. For counted cross stitch it's super simple to use and the worst that can happen is that it can knot. I recommend working with two strands for whole stitches (so dividing the original thread into three sets of two strands) and then working with lengths of around 30–50cm (12–20in), adjusting them on your needle to get started. For backstitch use a single strand.

In this book I have used DMC stranded cotton (floss), but there are many alternatives available and the conversion chart at the end of this book will help you to get the closest colour matches.

Using thread from well known brands is best from an environmental standpoint, as their manufacture is likely to be far less polluting than unbranded and cheaper flosses. Both DMC and Anchor threads are produced in accordance with Oeko-Tex® Standard 100, ensuring that flosses are free from banned azo dyes, as well as carcinogenic and allergenic dyestuffs.

Scissors

Good embroidery scissors are sharp and fine-pointed for cleanly cutting thread to the correct length, and for snipping off loose ends. To keep them sharp, never use them to cut paper or fabric. Instead you will need a separate pair of fabric scissors for cutting your Aida or linen.

Needles

Like most things, you can get by with needles that are too big or too small, but using a good embroidery needle that is the right size for the fabric will make stitching much quicker and easier. Tapestry needles are best for cross stitch because they have a rounded point so will not snag the fabric. However, always be careful with where they are left (please never, ever, cross stitch in bed!). A magnetic needle minder is a good idea to give you somewhere to 'park' your needle when it's not in use – there are many fun designs available.

Frames and hoops

Frames keep your fabric taut while working, can save you a huge amount of time and also ensure that your stitching is even. I like to keep it simple and use a bamboo hoop (which is also much better than a plastic one from an environmental standpoint) but there are many varieties available, including some really fancy ones that you don't even have to hold! Try out a few different models if you're unsure. A local craft store can be a good source of inspiration and advice here.

The heart is powerful. It is responsible for our strongest emotions – passion, fear, and most importantly, love. But it is also fragile and can be broken or damaged in a way that means opening your heart to others can sometimes be tough too. I interpret being brave in matters of the heart as embracing the risk that comes with giving and receiving love, and having faith that your heart will take you in the direction you're meant to go (even if it takes a strange route).

Info

- Stitch count: 129 x 200

- Stitched size (on 14-count Aida or 28-count linen): 23.4 x 36.3cm (9¼ x 14¼in)

Shopping List

- 1 skein of each DMC stranded cotton (floss) listed in the chart key. If a colour requires more than one skein the number needed is indicated in brackets after the colour.

- White Aida or linen, at least 38 x 52cm (15 x 20½in)

DMC
Stranded
cotton

Cross Stitch

⬤	347 (2)
Z	435
◆	603
⬆	761 (2)
⌐	3811
◣	422
⊐	598
✕	608 (2)
▼	815 (3)

Backstitch
— 815

DMC
Stranded
cotton

Cross Stitch

- ○ 347 (2)
- Z 435
- ◆ 603
- 761 (2)
- 3811
- 422
- 598
- 608 (2)
- ▼ 815 (3)

Backstitch

- — 815

It's true you don't need love to survive, but sharing and receiving love from others is a wonderful thing that brings something extra to life (often in a way that money and material possesions fail to do). Whether it's something little like suprising a friend you've not seen in a while or caring for someone unwell, all the way through to connecting with someone romantically and sharing your life with them. Experiencing and sharing these small and large acts of love is one of the sweetest parts of being human.

Info

· Stitch count: 100 x 99

· Stitched size (on 14-count Aida or 28-count linen): 18 x 18cm (7 x 7in)

Shopping List

· 1 skein of each DMC stranded cotton (floss) listed in the chart key

· Antique white Aida or linen, at least 33 x 33cm (13 x 13in)

Model stitched by Michelle Luscombe

DMC Stranded cotton

Cross Stitch

- 33
- 434
- · 726
- 898
- 3811
- 166
- 580
- 783
- 3608
- 3820

Backstitch

- 34
- 502
- 780
- 898
- 937

The ancient Greeks had different words for love, depending on the context – love for friends, romantic love and compassionate love were all understood to need their own name. Even now throughout the world, words for love vary widely as you can see in this design. However, the unspoken language of love is universal. It doesn't matter where you're from. Even if the words are different, 'love' is one thing we all have in common.

Info

- Stitch count: 142 x 129

- Stitched size (on 14-count Aida or 28-count linen): 25.8 x 23.4cm (10⅛ x 9¼in)

Shopping List

- 1 skein of each DMC stranded cotton (floss) listed in the chart key. If a colour requires more than one skein the number needed is indicated in brackets after the colour.

- Ecru Aida or linen, at least 46 x 43cm (18 x 17in)

Model stitched by Eleanor Cooper

DMC Stranded cotton

Cross Stitch

3848	
A	666
P	956
A	3341
	815 (2)
/	606 (2)
W	3811
1	604

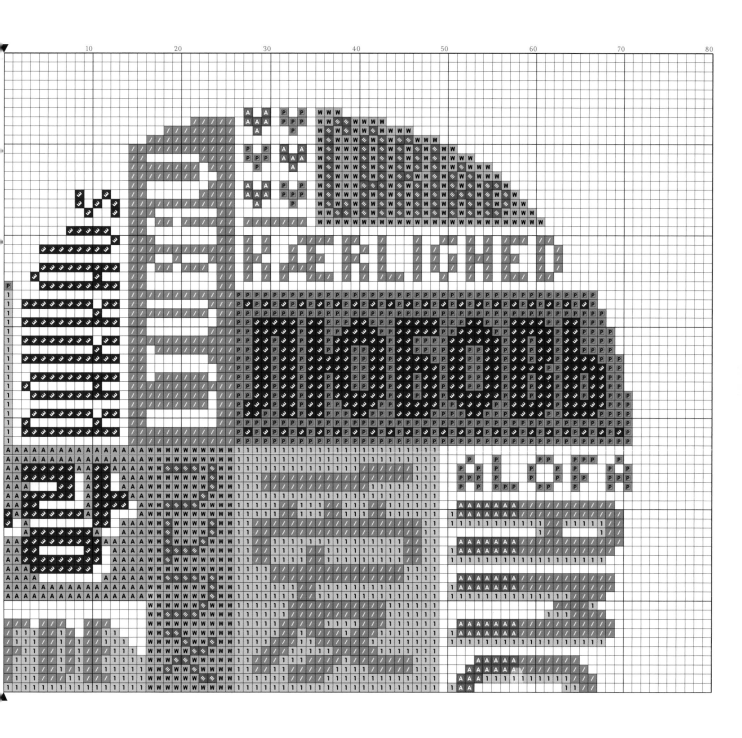

DMC Stranded cotton

Cross Stitch

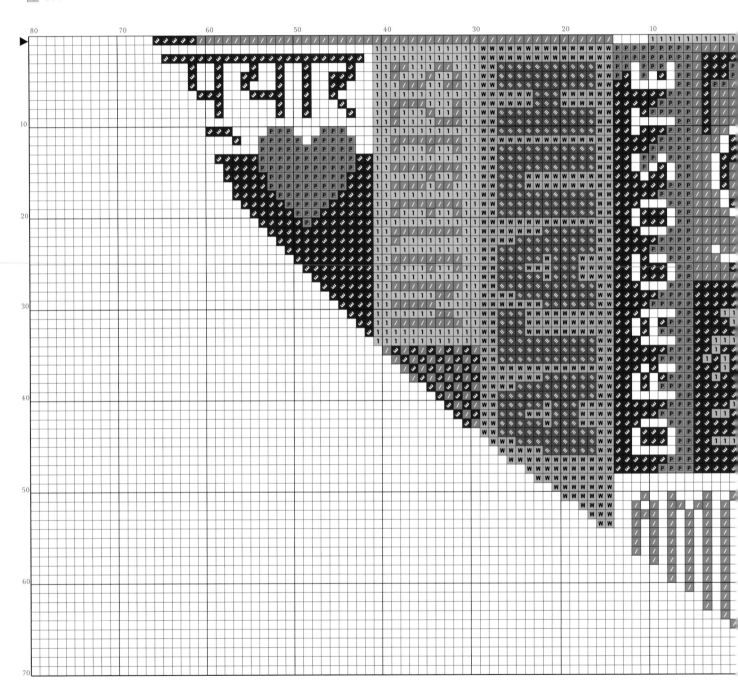

- 22 -

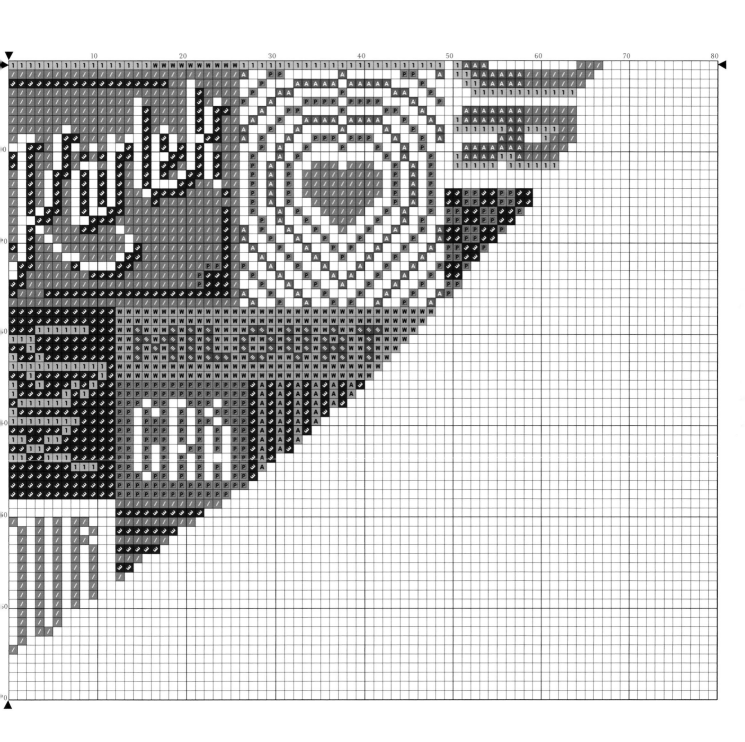

When you love someone, it's rarely because of one big thing, but rather a collection of lots of little things… favourite places, your song, things that make you both laugh and smile, as well as mutual respect, friendship and love towards each other. This sampler is a collection of tokens and trinkets to show this sweet side of love, which could be stitched together or individually.

Info
- Stitch count: 198 x 129
- Stitched size (on 14-count Aida or 28-count linen): 36 x 23.4cm (14 x 9¼in)

Shopping List
- 1 skein of each DMC stranded cotton (floss) listed in the chart key. If a colour requires more than one skein the number needed is indicated in brackets after the colour.

- White Aida or linen, at least 51 x 38cm (20 x 15in)

Model stitched by Eleanor Cooper

DMC
Stranded
cotton

Cross Stitch

↑ 225 (2)
✕ 352 (2)
▼ 519
C 603
◆ 816 (2)
▬ 3761 (2)
✕ 351
◤ 472
⋈ 602
★ 604
▬ 832
⊢ ECRU

Backstitch

— 351
— 602
— 816
— 3761

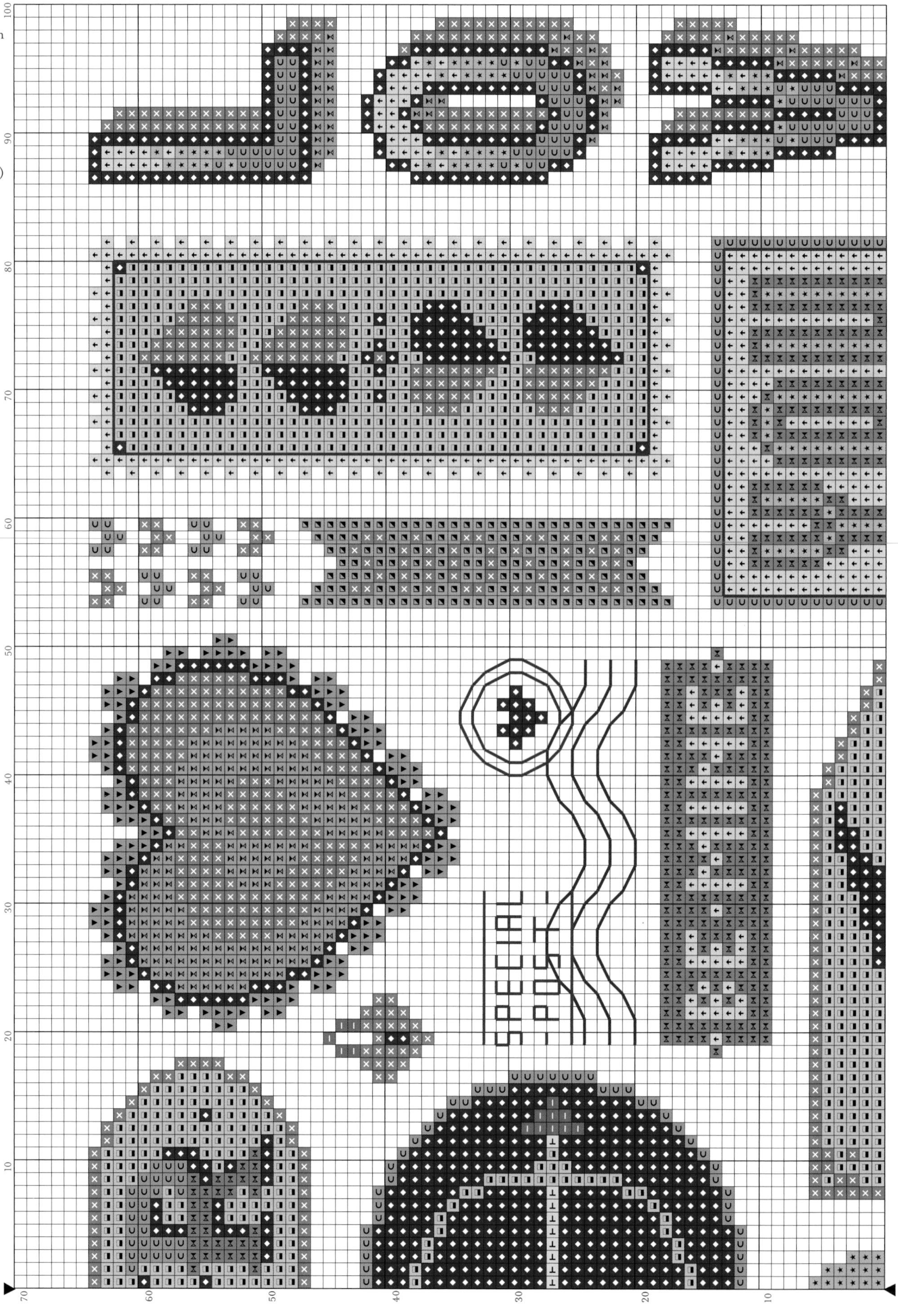

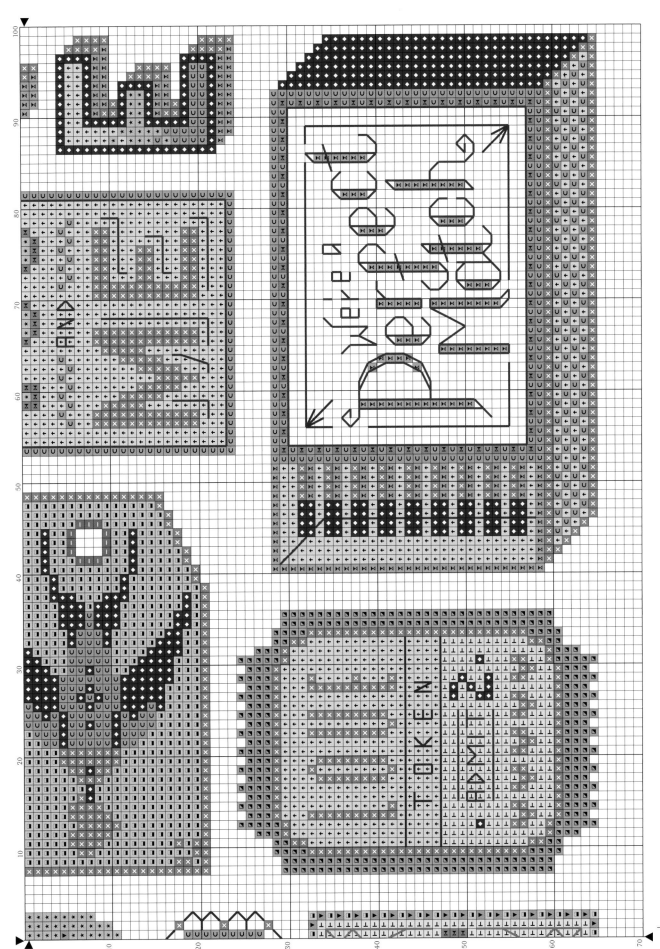

DMC
Stranded
cotton

Cross Stitch

Symbol	Colour
↑	225 (2)
✕	352 (2)
▼	519
C	603
◆	816 (2)
▬	3761 (2)
✕	351
◩	472
⋈	602
★	604
▬	832
⊢	ECRU

Backstitch

Symbol	Colour
▬	351
▬	602
▬	816
▬	3761

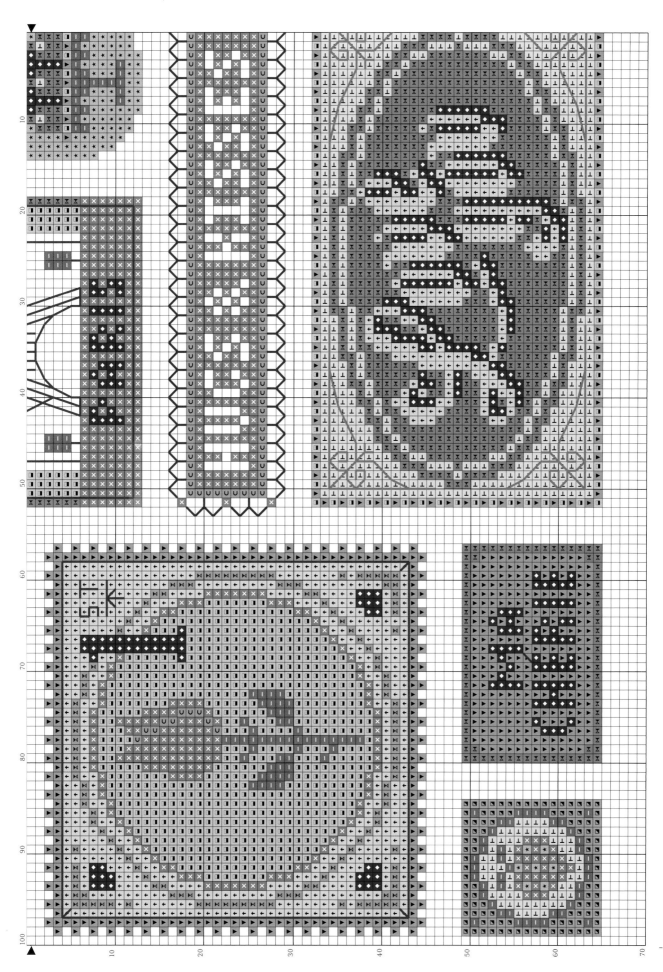

Loving someone completely means accepting every part of them and all the while acknowledging that these elements make up who they are and why you love them. We don't know what will happen in the future – that's what makes life interesting – but knowing that your love will always be there for those you hold close, wherever life takes them, is a wonderful thing to share.

Info
- Stitch count: 73 x 130
- Stitched size (on 14-count Aida or 28-count linen): 13.5 x 23.4cm (5¼ x 9¼in)

Shopping List
- 1 skein of each DMC stranded cotton (floss) listed in the chart key
- Blush Aida or linen, at least 33 x 44.5cm (13 x 17½in)

Model stitched by Eleanor Cooper

DMC
Stranded
cotton

Cross Stitch

O	3777
◢	598
=	819
◪	3706
◯	3708

Backstitch

— 3777
— 3706

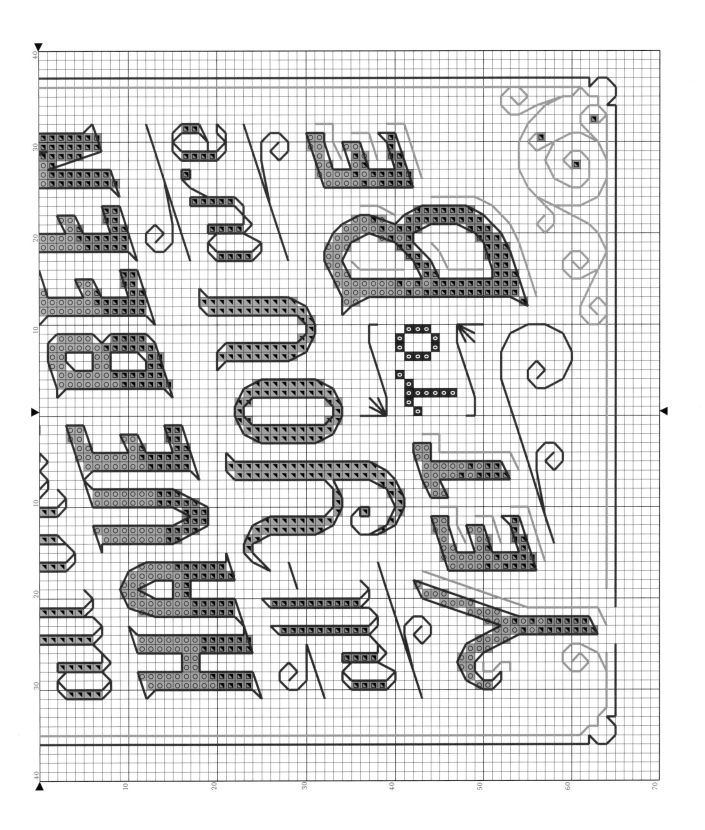

This quote by E.E Cummings is such a lovely way to think about those we love the most. I created this design with my daughter in mind, as she was born during the making of this book. Of course, there are no rules about who you can apply this sentiment to in your own life – partners, family, pets and friends can all take up huge parts of our hearts in ways we could never imagine.

Info
- Stitch count: 128 x 176
- Stitched size (on 14-count Aida or 28-count linen): 23.1 x 32cm (9⅛ x 12⅝in)

Shopping List
- 1 skein of each DMC stranded cotton (floss) listed in the chart key. If a colour requires more than one skein the number needed is indicated in brackets after the colour.
- White Aida or linen, at least 43.1 x 52cm (17 x 20½in)

Model stitched by Michelle Luscombe

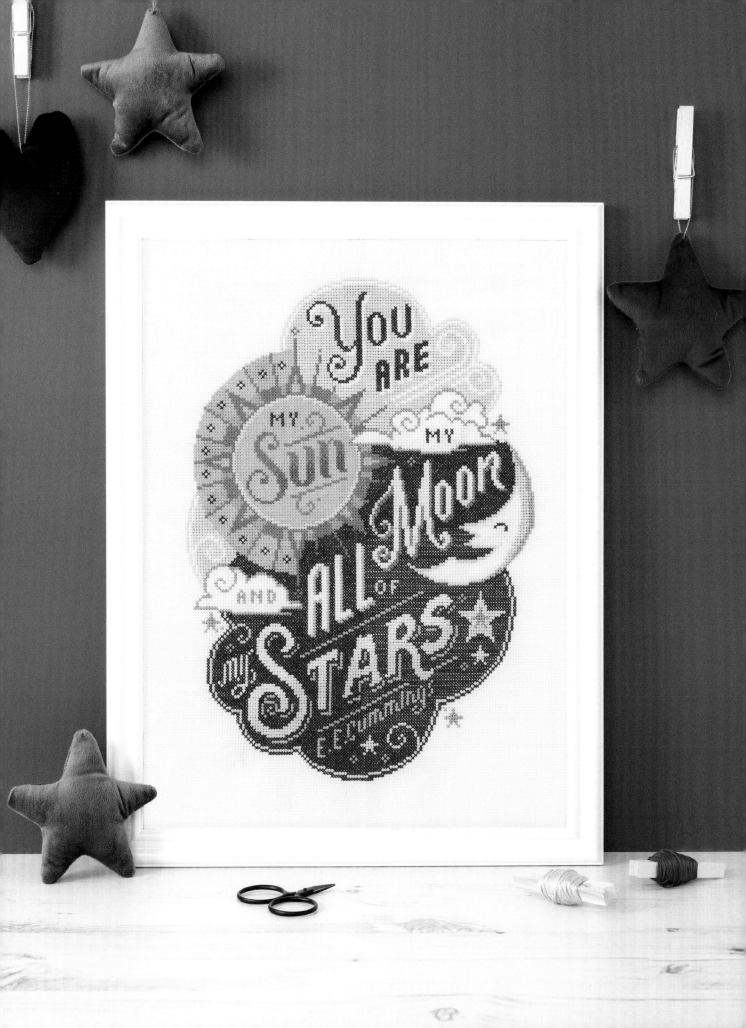

DMC
Stranded
cotton

Cross Stitch

N	25
⌴	340
◈	721
◣	728
⬇	819
5	956
8	3747
◥	318
⊢	341
F	726
O	792 (4)
C	921
◈	957
J	3761 (2)

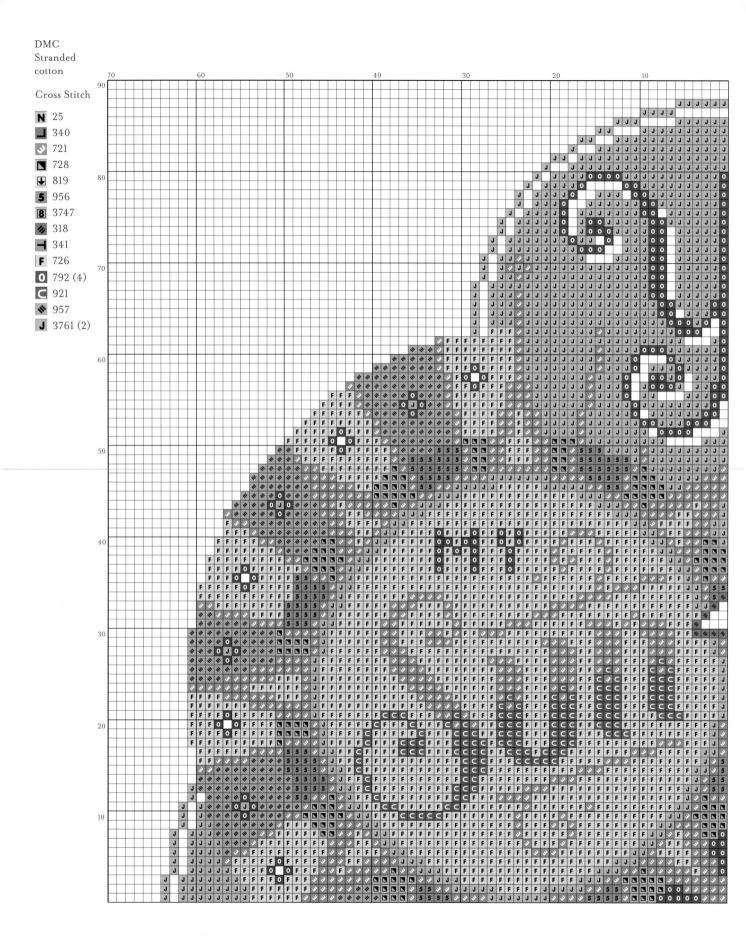

DMC
Stranded
cotton

Cross Stitch

N	25
◢	340
◈	721
◣	728
⤓	819
5	956
8	3747
◧	318
⊣	341
F	726
0	792 (4)
C	921
◈	957
J	3761 (2)

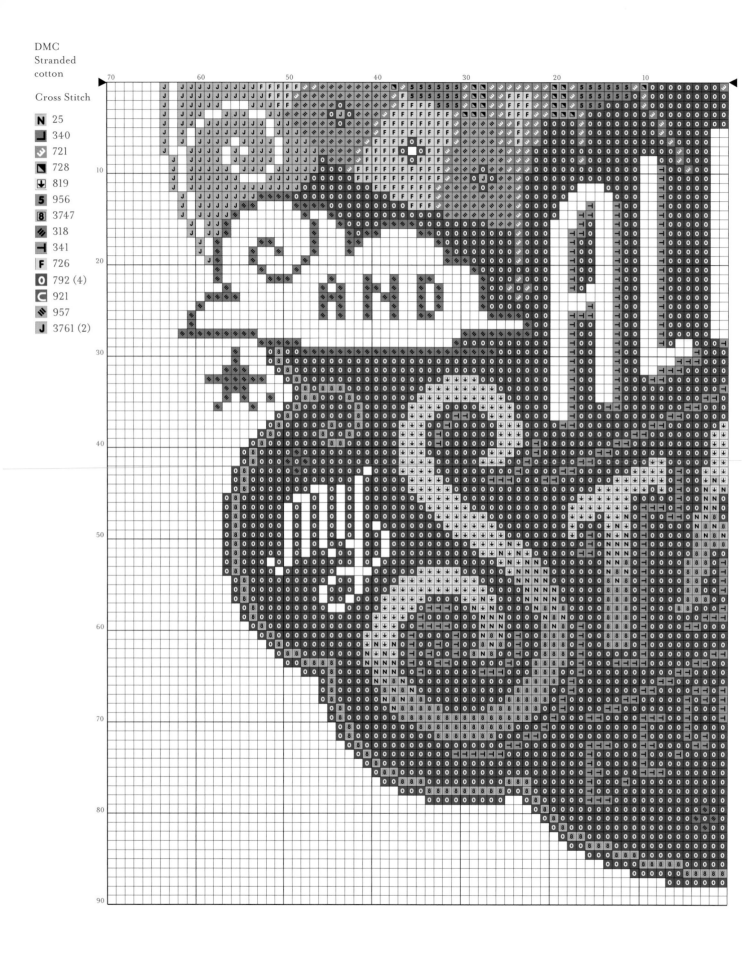

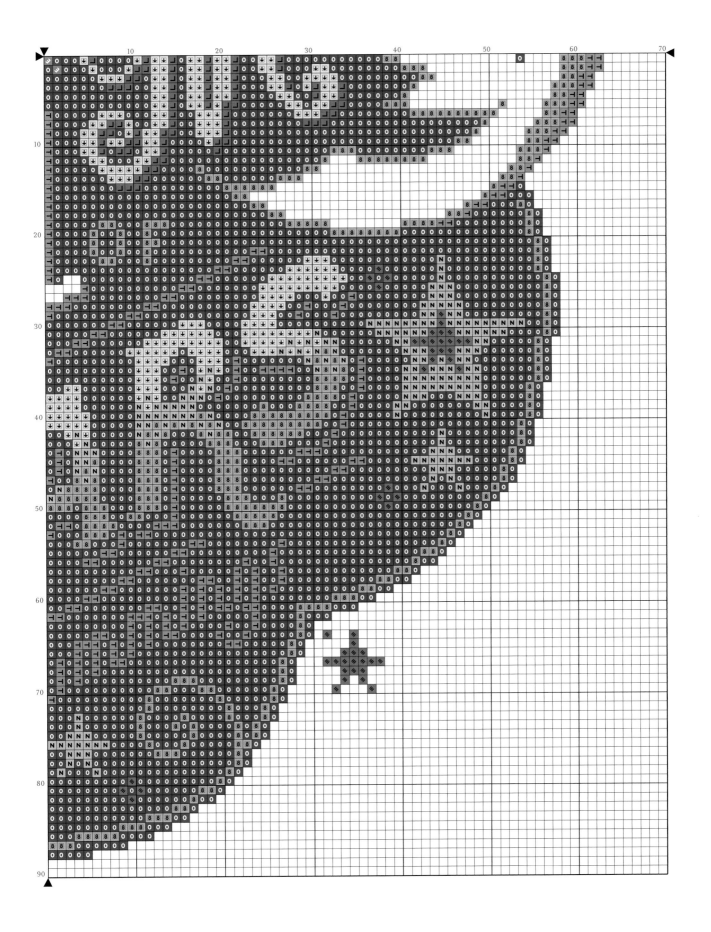

Family comes in all shapes and sizes, and has evolved to mean more than just relationships by blood and marriage. It also means the people in your life who support and love you, those you can confide in and trust; those you are closest to and whom you can depend on without judgement, who share your values. Some of my oldest friends are family to me, and I hope I'm family to them.

Info

- Stitch count: 131 x 200

- Stitched size (on 14-count Aida or 28-count linen): 23.8 x 36.1cm (9⅜ x 14¼in)

Shopping List

- 1 skein of each DMC stranded cotton (floss) listed in the chart key

- Antique White Aida or linen, at least 44.4 x 57.1cm (17½ x 22½in)

Model stitched by Michelle Luscombe

DMC
Stranded
cotton

Cross Stitch

C 434
U 721
→ 956
D 959
◑ 964
⬆ 3819
★ 436
U 501
◣ 722
S 957
6 963
� 3705
< 3849

Backstitch

— 434
— 436
— 501
— 3705

Cross Stitch

C	434
U	721
➜	956
D	959
◐	964
⬆	3819
★	436
U	501
◢	722
S	957
6	963
◈	3705
C	3849

Backstitch

—	434
—	436
—	501
—	3705

Time spent with those you love is precious. We all lead busy lives so being able to pause and just enjoy being in each other's company without distraction can be easy to forget. This pattern is very personal to me as one of my favourite places to be is with my beautiful cats, either chilling in the garden or curled up on the sofa. I know there are a lot of cat owners amongst the stitching community, so I hope this resonates with you too.

Info

- Stitch count: 92 x 128

- Stitched size (on 14-count Aida or 28-count linen): 16.8 x 23.1cm (6⅝ x 9⅛in)

Shopping List

- 1 skein of each DMC stranded cotton (floss) listed in the chart key

- White Aida or linen, at least 36.8 x 43.1cm (14½ x 17in)

Model stitched by Sandra Doolan

Cross Stitch

↓	312
−	3755
C	3325
◠	322
◿	775
/	B5200

Backstitch

—	312
—	322
—	3325

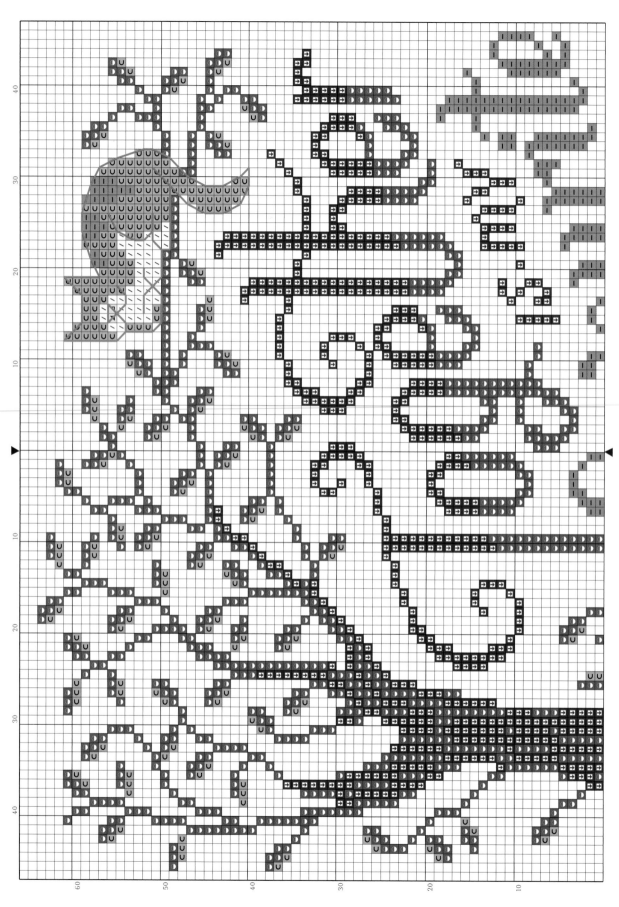

We are told we can do so much with our lives but it's easy to overlook the things that are actually important to basic happiness. Things such as practising compassion and kindness, and being careful not to judge (particularly based on what we read online). Being kind costs nothing, yet it can bring so much to others in terms of happiness. It also makes you feel good knowing that you've brought a little joy to someone else's day.

Info

- Stitch count: 89 x 130

- Stitched size (on 14-count Aida or 28-count linen): 16.5 x 23.5cm (6⅜ x 8⅝in)

Shopping List

- 1 skein of each DMC stranded cotton (floss) listed in the chart key

- White Aida or linen, at least 37 x 42cm (14½ x 16½in)

Model stitched by Glenda Dickson

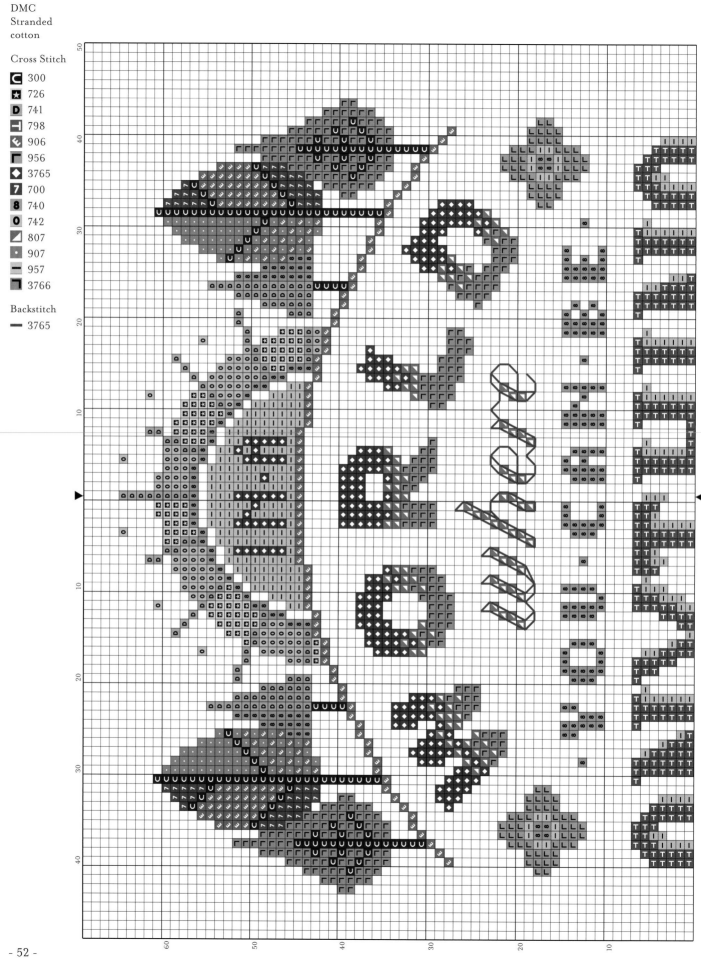

DMC
Stranded
cotton

Cross Stitch

C	300
★	726
D	741
⊣	798
◆	906
⌐	956
◇	3765
7	700
8	740
0	742
◢	807
•	907
—	957
⌐	3766

Backstitch

—	3765

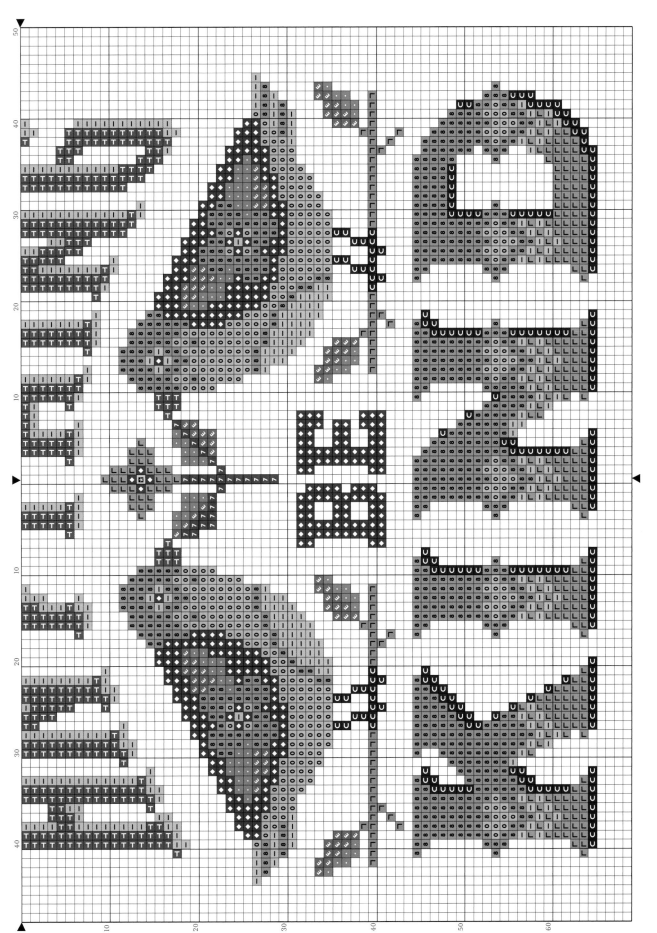

It's safe to say that many measure their success from a materialistic perspective. However, history judges us for our actions more than our wealth. Sharing your love, time, skills or possessions with others can transform lives in ways that you might not even realize. Helping causes that you are passionate about is a great thing to do both for yourself and for the wider world.

Info

· Stitch count: 102 x 130

· Stitched size (on 14-count Aida or 28-count linen): 18.5 x 23cm (7¼ x 9¼in)

Shopping List

· 1 skein of each DMC stranded cotton (floss) listed in the chart key

· Ivory Aida or linen, at least 39.5 x 44.5cm (15½ x 17½in)

Model stitched by Michelle Luscombe

DMC
Stranded
cotton

Cross Stitch

◈	35
▼	722
⋈	957
✕	970
⬇	3804
⟱	721
○	741
7	963
⊥	3761
⟴	3809

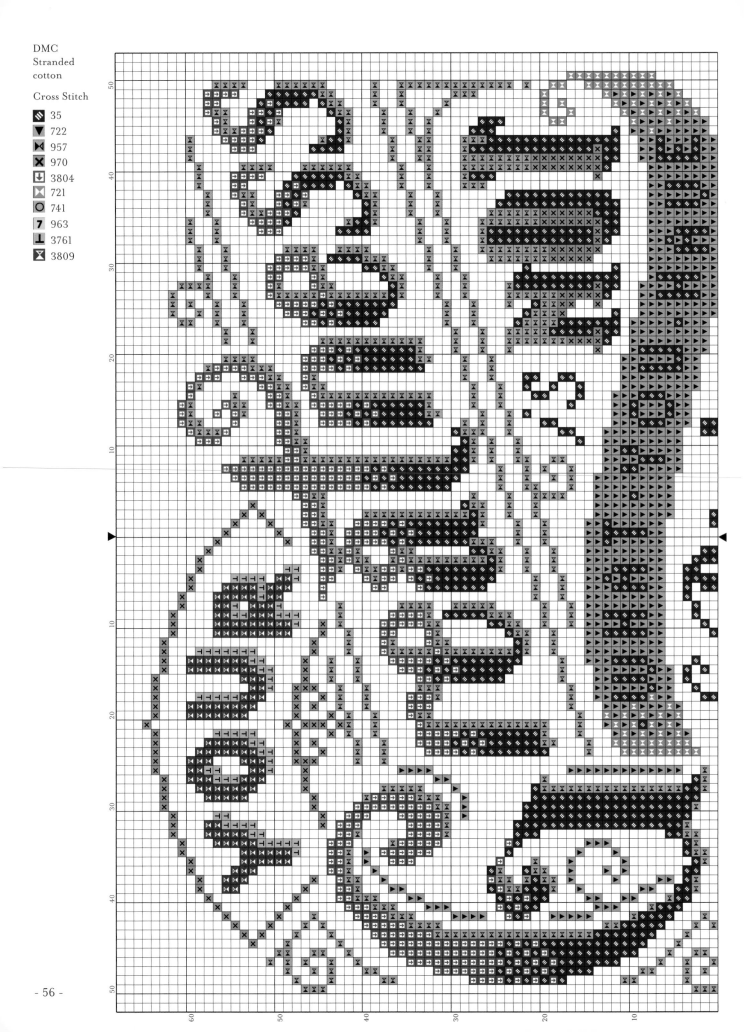

I know from experience that just one kind gesture can make someone's day. In tough times something as simple as a chat with a neighbour or a text from a friend has been the thing I needed to boost my day. These interactions are even more important for those who live alone – loneliness is widespread even in our populated world. Remember that little connections can be just as significant as big gestures, especially for anyone having a hard time.

Info
- Stitch count: 93 x 130
- Stitched size (on 14-count Aida or 28-count linen): 16.8 x 23.4cm (6⅝ x 9¼in)

Shopping List
- 1 skein of each DMC stranded cotton (floss) listed in the chart key
- Pale cream Aida or linen, at least 36.8 x 44.4cm (14½ x 17½in)

Model stitched by Kirsty Torrance

Cross Stitch

◩	169
✚	517
⧖	718
◠	947
⊥	973
⬆	996
◣	775
◇	311
7	605
◀	741
◆	956
⬇	995
V	3607

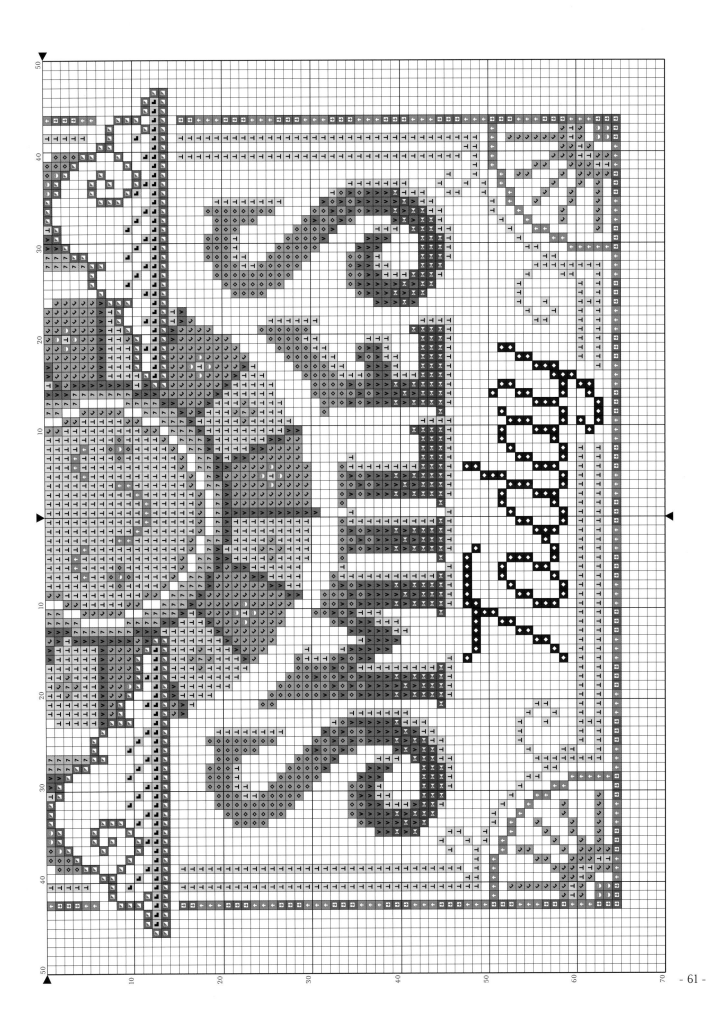

Sometimes we need an encouraging and understanding friend to give us a boost. And sometimes, we need to be that person for someone else. We are social animals after all, designed to be with others and benefit from their company. By spreading some positivity, kindness and compassion in the lives of others, we gain more purpose in our own existence so that ultimately everyone wins.

Info

- Stitch count: 100 x 129

- Stitched size (on 14-count Aida or 28-count linen): 18 x 23.5cm (7⅛ x 9¼in)

Shopping List

- 1 skein of each DMC stranded cotton (floss) listed in the chart key

- White Aida or linen, at least 38 x 43.2cm (15 x 17in)

Model stitched by Glenda Dickson

DMC
Stranded
cotton

Cross Stitch

4	597
↑	721
\	741
9	920
⋈	3727
◿	3810
F	598
8	726
7	775
F	963
0	3808
F	3825

Backstitch
— 3808

French Knots
• 3808

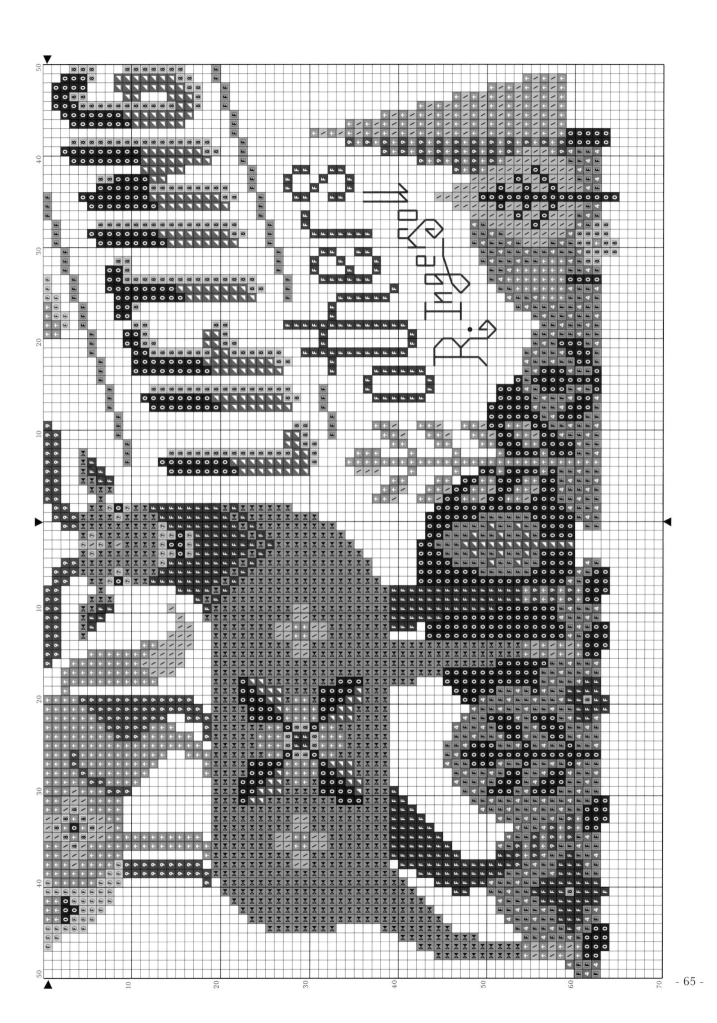

There are so many acts of kindness that we can weave into our daily lives. They don't always have to be grand gestures (though these are great too). Being mindful of those around us is a great place to start, and it's a lovely feeling to have made someone smile by doing something kind for them. Even if it's as simple as holding a door open or offering a seat, it'll be appreciated.

Info

· Stitch count: 127 x 198

· Stitched size (on 14-count Aida or 28-count linen): 23.1 x 35.8cm (9⅛ x 14⅛in)

Shopping List

· 1 skein of each DMC stranded cotton (floss) listed in the chart key. If a colour requires more than one skein the number needed is indicated in brackets after the colour.

· White Aida or linen, at least 43.1 x 55.8cm (17 x 22in)

Model stitched by Nicola Gravener

DMC
Stranded
cotton

Cross Stitch

☑ 3834 (4)
╱ 352 (2)
◙ 318
◖ 3835
∩ 3609
◩ 3608

Backstitch
— 352
— 3834
— 3608

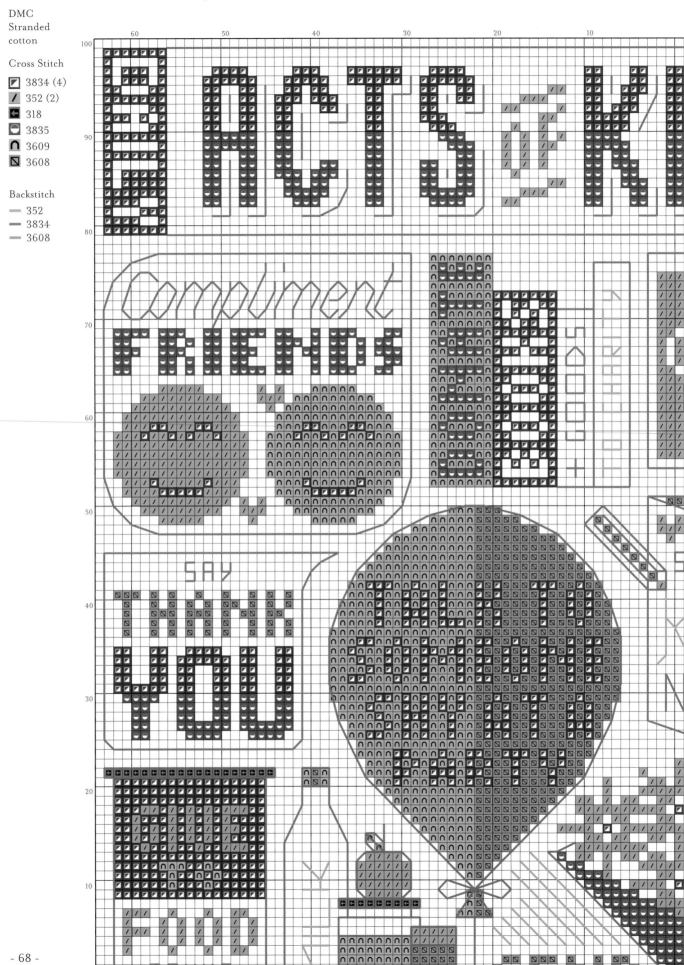

DMC
Stranded
cotton

Cross Stitch

⬕ 3834 (4)
◪ 352 (2)
⬕ 318
⬕ 3835
∩ 3609
⬕ 3608

Backstitch
— 352
— 3834
— 3608

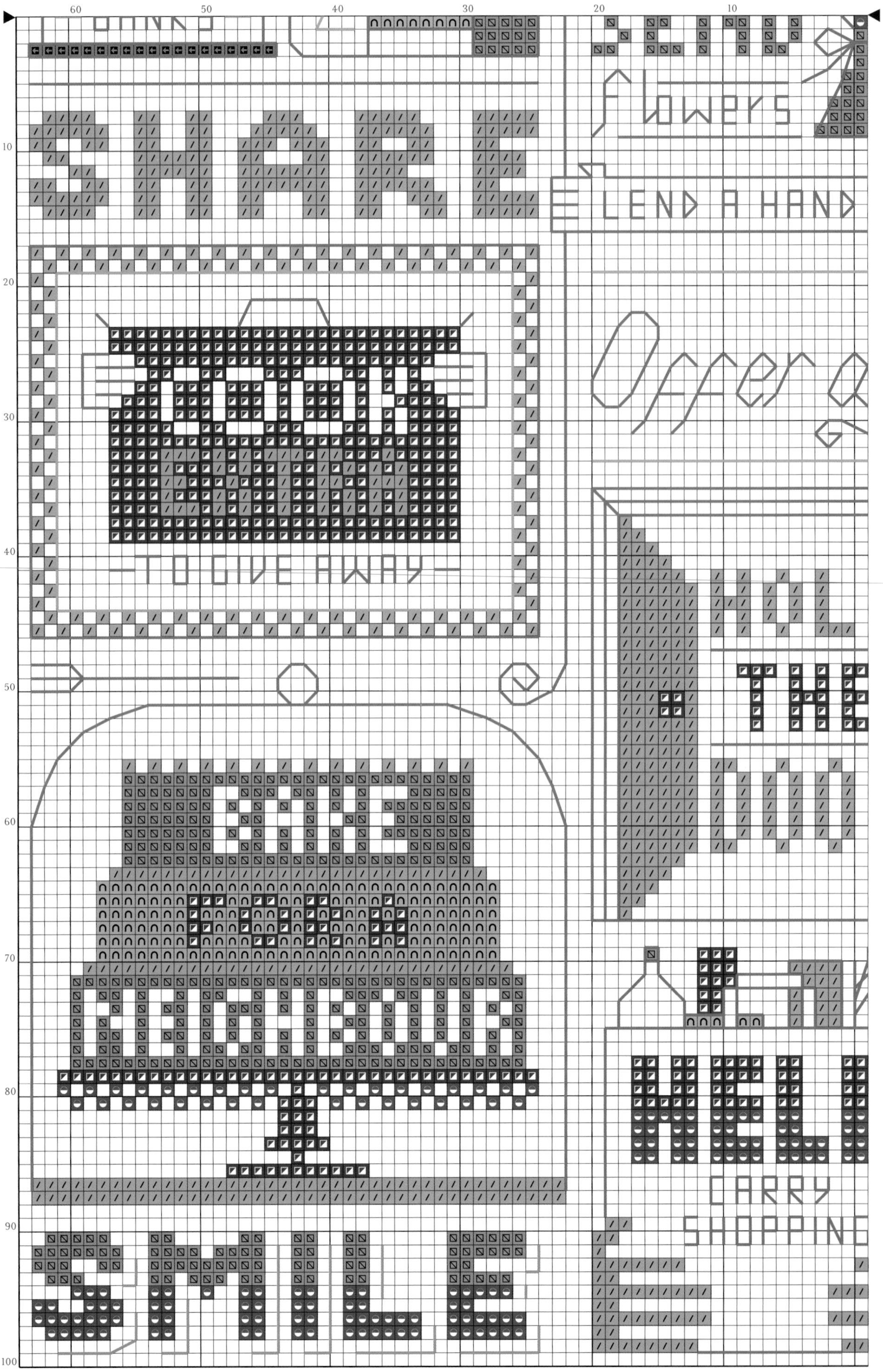

We live in a competitive world and it's easy to compare ourselves to others in work, life and love. Actually there are no rules for what you should be doing in life, and when. Being happy is the essential thing. So we should encourage each other in all our endeavours – work or hobbies, or within our families. Passions can easily be dampened, but supporting people in what they enjoy helps them lead happier lives.

Info

- Stitch count: 99 x 130

- Stitched size (on 14-count Aida or 28-count linen): 18 x 23.4cm (7⅛ x 9¼in)

Shopping List

- 1 skein of each DMC stranded cotton (floss) listed in the chart key

- Platinum Aida or linen, at least 38 x 44.4cm (15 x 17½in)

Model stitched by Sandra Doolan

DMC
Stranded
cotton

Cross Stitch

E	18
✚	34
◄	341
◩	503
▽	597
⌐	961
7	3809
◲	33
◺	166
←	502
▼	580
C	793
A	3354
✎	3810

- 74 -

We all need a hug and some TLC every so often. This may feel like an obvious statement, but it's worth remembering. However strong people appear on the outside, deep down they may still be craving a caring cuddle. Hugs are great for the giver too! They are proven to lower stress, increase our wellbeing and even help fight infection. So more hugs please!

Info
- Stitch count: 100 x 100
- Stitched size (on 14-count Aida or 28-count linen): 18 x 18cm (7⅛ x 7⅛in)

Shopping List
- 1 skein of each DMC stranded cotton (floss) listed in the chart key
- Navy Aida or linen, at least 38 x 38cm (15 x 15in)

Model stitched by Michelle Luscombe

◩	310
◪	597
◉	3350
8	3731
⬇	3756
☐	3811
D	352
✿	842
N	3354
★	3733
✕	3809

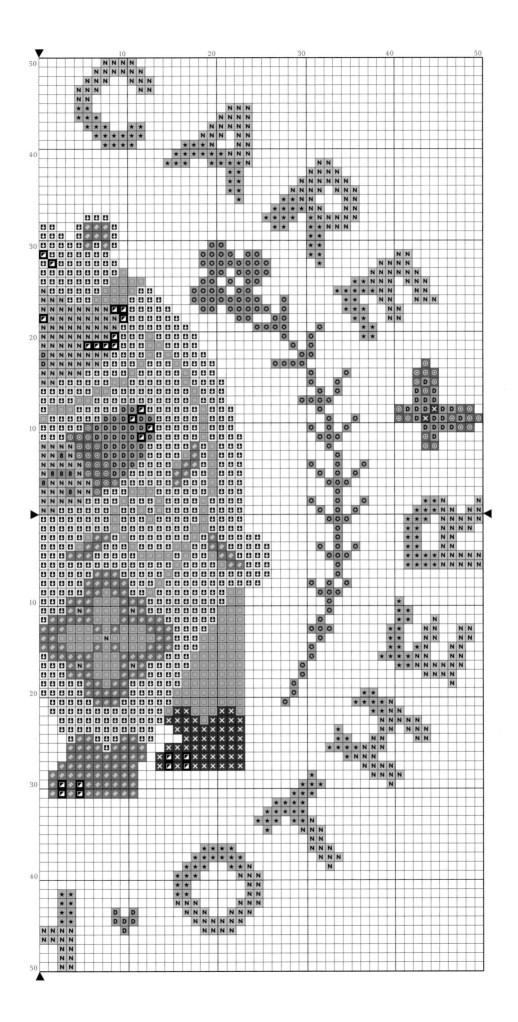

We all need little messages of love and support from others occasionally, especially if life has thrown us a few knocks or made us doubt how much we are cared for. These little hoops are ideal for gifts and can be easily turned into cards to send to someone you're thinking of, or who might benefit from a reminder of love and kindness.

Info
- You are very special to me, stitch count: 65 x 60; stitched size: 11.7 x 10.7cm (4⅝ x 4¼in)

- You are so loved, stitch count: 66 x 65; stitched size: 12 x 11.7cm (4¾ x 4⅝in)

Shopping List
- 1 skein of each DMC stranded cotton (floss) listed in the chart key

- White Aida or linen, at least 34.2 x 31.7cm (13½ x 12½in)

- Hoop size: 15cm (6in)

Models stitched by Sharon Atkinson

DMC Stranded cotton

Cross Stitch

D	340	★	352
→	603	⊃	963
⑥	973	⊔	3746
⊣	3841	▽	355

Backstitch
— 355
— 603
— 3746

DMC Stranded cotton

Cross Stitch

D	340	↙	351
★	352	→	603
A	604	⊃	963
⑥	973	Ц	3746
⊣	3841	▽	355

Backstitch
— 352
— 355
— 3746

It's easy to rely on others to make you feel good, especially in the age of social media. Seeking and obtaining validation from others can make us feel better in the short term, but being kind and loving to *yourself* is also vital to long-term happiness. After all, it's hard to be happy when your own mind is filled with self-doubt. Our differences are one of the best things about being human, so we should embrace ourselves just as we are.

Info
- Stitch count: 100 x 100
- Stitched size (on 14-count Aida or 28-count linen): 18 x 18cm (7⅛ x 7⅛in)

Shopping List
- 1 skein of each DMC stranded cotton (floss) listed in the chart key
- Ivory Aida or linen, at least 38 x 38cm (15 x 15in)

Model stitched by Sharon Atkinson

DMC
Stranded
cotton

Cross Stitch

◈	355
◤	600
◉	957
A	3705
◢	3824
★	597
⊔	951
↑	959
↓	3747
◆	3839

Backstitch

—	355
—	797
—	3705
—	3814

I've wanted to create a pattern specifically for Pride and the LGBT+ movement for a while. We should all be able to live our lives without judgement or fear – in terms of who we love and who we are. Festivals celebrating Pride are a riot of flamboyant colour but amidst the celebrations they're also campaigning for everyone's right to live their lives on a genuinely equal footing.

Info

· Stitch count: 200 x 130

· Stitched size (on 14-count Aida or 28-count linen): 36.1 x 23.4cm (14¼ x 9¼in)

Shopping List

· 1 skein of each DMC stranded cotton (floss) listed in the chart key. If a colour requires more than one skein the number needed is indicated in brackets after the colour.

· White Aida or linen, at least 57.1 x 44.4cm (22½ x 17½in)

Model stitched by Michelle Luscombe

DMC
Stranded
cotton

Cross Stitch

1	E168
→	444 (2)
⊥	608 (2)
◔	740
≋	907
0	956 (2)
4	972
◇	3845 (2)
◯	208
◈	550
⊓	666
◢	827
◪	943 (2)
✕	957
✚	3809
◩	312 (2)

Backstitch

— 312

DMC
Stranded
cotton

Cross Stitch

Symbol	Color
1	E168
→	444 (2)
⊥	608 (2)
◖	740
◈	907
O	956 (2)
4	972
◇	3845 (2)
◯	208
◿	550
⌐	666
◢	827
◨	943 (2)
⊠	957
✚	3809
◪	312 (2)

Backstitch
— 312

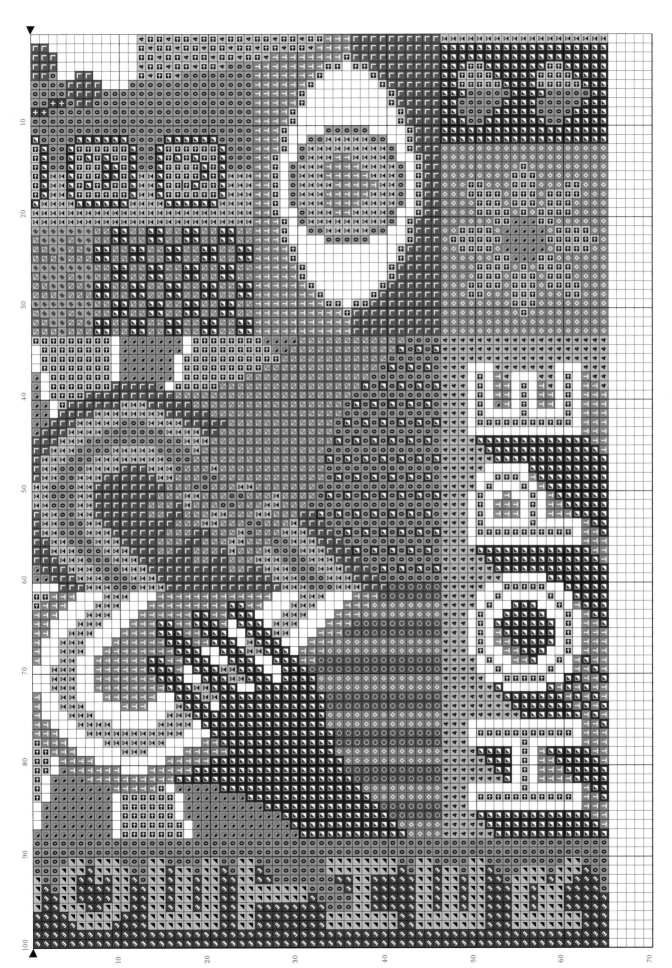

Grief can be crushing, whether the loss is a family member, friend or beloved pet. I wanted to create a pattern that commemorated all those we have said goodbye to in a way that's full of peace and love, rather than dwelling on the sadness or pain; even though we naturally feel those too. This Inuit proverb makes me think of all the loved ones I've lost in my life being together and happy, looking down, knowing we're always thinking of them.

Info

- Stitch count: 109 x 199

- Stitched size (on 14-count Aida or 28-count linen): 19.75 x 36cm (7¾ x 14¼in)

Shopping List

- 1 skein of each DMC stranded cotton (floss) listed in the chart key

- Navy Aida or linen, at least 35.5 x 51cm (14 x 20in)

Model stitched by Glenda Dickson

PERHAPS THEY·ARE Not STARS BUT·RATHER
OPENINGS IN HEAVEN LOVE ·OF·OUR
WHERE·THE· LOST ONES
POURS THROUGH & Shines down upon us
TO LET US KNOW THEY·ARE HAPPY

- Inuit Proverb -

DMC
Stranded
cotton

Cross Stitch

☙	24
➊	31
T	151
6	747
▣	3354
◣	3824
⌐	3733
5	26
★	32
◢	519
➷	948
➔	3752
◖	3865

Backstitch

—	30
—	519
—	3733
—	3752
—	3824
—	3865

- 96 -

DMC
Stranded
cotton

Cross Stitch

❤	24
◗	31
T	151
6	747
▢	3354
◣	3824
⌐	3733
5	26
★	32
◢	519
↘	948
→	3752
◖	3865

Backstitch

—	30
—	519
—	3733
—	3752
—	3824
—	3865

I thought this would be a great pattern to finish the book. To me, following your heart isn't just about taking risks and trusting your gut-instinct in matters of love, but also about following your passions and desires in other areas of life too. It comes with a risk, but if we always did what was sensible and practical life would be a lot less fun! So be the queen of your own heart.

Info
- Stitch count: 129 x 200
- Stitched size (on 14-count Aida or 28-count linen): 23.5 x 36.1cm (9¼ x 14¼in)

Shopping List
- 1 skein of each DMC stranded cotton (floss) listed in the chart key. If a colour requires more than one skein the number needed is indicated in brackets after the colour.
- White Aida or linen, at least 43.2 x 57.1cm (17 x 22½in)

Model stitched by Eleanor Cooper

DMC
Stranded
cotton

Cross Stitch

U	166
	815 (3)
A	3706
	3801
	353
T	963
	3708 (2)
J	3811 (2)

DMC
Stranded
cotton

Cross Stitch

U	166
	815 (3)
A	3706
	3801
	353
T	963
	3708 (2)
J	3811 (2)

Techniques

Preparing the Fabric

Always begin by ensuring that you have a piece of fabric large enough for your design. Make sure there is a good amount of clearance around the edge to allow for framing – I recommend at least 10cm (4in) on each side. To find the centre of the Aida fabric, fold the fabric in half and then in half again. Mark the centre point with a needle.

It's rubbish getting halfway through a piece and realizing the edges of your fabric are getting all frayed and tatty. A good way to avoid this is to use a zigzag stitch on a sewing machine to keep your edges tidy. If you don't have a sewing machine, fear not! Masking tape folded over all of the sides is an easy alternative. Just remember to add a little extra fabric to the area if you plan to do this, as you will need to chop it off before washing.

Cross Stitch

Once you've got the hang of this, the rest is a doddle! Working with two strands of thread in your needle, start your first cross stitch in the centre of the design and the centre of your fabric. You can stitch in rows by colour or individually depending on your preference (I tend to mix and match, depending on how I'm feeling).

To start, bring the needle up through the back of the fabric, leaving a 2cm (1in) tail of thread behind, which you should secure with your subsequent stitches. Take the needle back down through the fabric, creating a diagonal stitch, making sure that the thread tail at the back stays in place. Keep doing this until you have finished a

row (1), and then come back the other way, crossing the stitches diagonally to complete the row (2). Try to keep the top stitches running in the same direction if possible, as it creates a neater finish.

Continue to stitch until you have finished a section in that colour. At the end of the last cross stitch, the needle should be at the back of the fabric. Thread the needle through the back of four or five stitches to secure the thread, then cut away any excess.

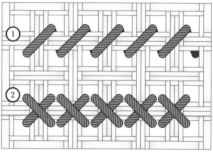

Making a row of cross stitch on Aida

Completed cross stitch on Aida

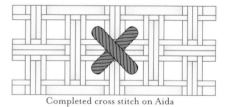

Making a row of cross stitch on linen

Completed cross stitch on linen

Backstitch

This stitch is ideal for adding detail, but it can be less forgiving than cross stitch. For backstitch, you should use a single strand of thread.

To start, bring the needle up through the fabric at the point of the first stitch, leaving a 2cm (1in) tail at the back, which you should secure with your subsequent stitches. Bring the needle back through the fabric at the point where the stitch will finish to create one backstitch. Next, bring the needle up at the point where the next stitch will finish and back down through the point where the first stitch starts. Continue until all of the backstitches in the chosen area have been completed.

French Knots

Start by bringing your needle up through your fabric where you need the knot and pull the thread through. Now holding the thread taut with your left hand, take it behind the needle which is held in your right hand (which you keep still). Use your left hand to wrap the thread twice round the needle keeping the thread taut. Then push the needle back down through the fabric close to the hole which you used to begin with. Slide the knot down the needle until it reaches the fabric then pull the floss underneath until a knot forms and securely anchor the back.

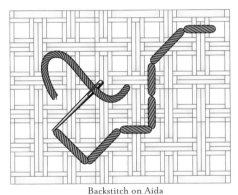

Backstitch on Aida

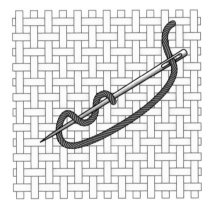

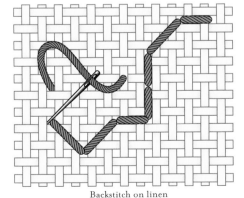

Backstitch on linen

Stitch Count and Design Size

For each design in this book I have given the finished size and stitch count based on the type of fabric and size of weave that I have used. It is important to note that if you choose an alternative count of fabric it will change the finished design size.

To work out the size of your final design, first work out the stitch count (if it has not already been given). Do this by counting the number of stitches along the width of the design and then the number along the height. Each number should then be divided by the count of the fabric you're using in order to give you the width and height in inches.

For Aida fabric the count represents the number of threads per inch. For linen it's the same but, because you stitch over two threads rather than one, divide the count by two before making your calculations.

For example, if the finished size is given as 120 w x 140 h on 16-count fabric (or 32-count linen):

· 120 divided by 16 = 7½in

· 140 divided by 16 = 8¾in

· The final design size is 7½ x 8¾in

There are plenty of calculators available online if your brain feels like it has turned to mush at this point!

Following Charts

Charts are made up of multiple coloured squares, each featuring symbols, which refer to a chart key. Here's a handy guide:

· Each coloured square represents a whole cross stitch.

· The symbols relate to specific thread colours and should be cross-referenced against the key at the side of the chart.

· Single lines of colour represent backstitches, and are also shown in thread colours in the key.

· French knots are indicated by a dot.

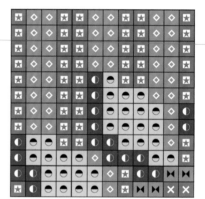

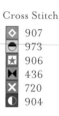

Cross Stitch

◇	907
◖	973
✪	906
◄	436
✕	720
◑	904

Cleaning

Always hand wash your work with a delicate detergent in warm water. Do not rub or wring, but rather soak and gently agitate after a few minutes. Rinse well in cold water and allow to dry flat. I'm always terrified to wash pieces, but as long as you've used good quality, branded stranded cotton and colourfast fabric you should have no issues with colours running. When you're ready to iron, place a towel on your ironing board and then iron your piece right side down over this, using a hot steam setting. *Et voila!*

Framing

There are so many options for framing embroidery these days, so feel free to choose what works for you. I sometimes just use a simple hoop, which is laced from the back. This inexpensive method of framing is perfect for creating multiple designs for a feature wall. You can also paint the hoops or wrap them with ribbon for added pops of complementary colour.

Throughout this book I have used a few different framing options to demonstrate the various effects you can create. Take a look through the pages and choose your favourite – you may decide to replicate the method I've chosen for a particular design or to try something new.

Conversion Chart

I have used DMC thread; however, if you prefer, you can use Anchor, which is just as good. This conversion chart shows all the colours used in this book.

DMC	Anchor	DMC	Anchor	DMC	Anchor	DMC	Anchor	DMC	Anchor
18	295	355	1014	726	295	947	330	3747	120
24	103	422	934	728	305	948	1011	3752	1032
25	103	434	310	740	316	951	1010	3755	939
26	342	435	1046	741	304	956	40	3756	1037
30	118	436	1045	742	303	957	50	3761	928
31	122	444	290	747	158	959	186	3765	170
32	123	472	253	761	1021	961	76	3766	167
33	92	501	878	775	128	963	73	3777	1015
34	94	502	877	780	309	964	185	3801	1098
35	94	503	876	783	306	970	316	3804	63
151	73	517	162	792	177	972	298	3808	1068
166	254	519	1038	793	176	973	297	3809	1066
168 (E168*)	234	550	101	797	132	995	410	3810	1066
169	849	580	281	798	131	996	433	3811	1060
208	111	597	1064	807	168	3325	129	3814	1074
225	1026	598	1062	815	22	3341	328	3819	253
300	352	600	59	816	20	3350	59	3820	306
310	403	602	57	819	271	3354	74	3824	8
311	148	603	62	827	160	3607	87	3834	100
312	979	604	55	832	907	3608	86	3835	98
318	399	605	1094	842	1080	3609	85	3839	176
322	978	606	334	898	360	3705	35	3841	9159
340	118	608	332	906	256	3706	33	3845	1089
341	117	666	46	907	255	3708	31	3848	1074
347	1025	700	211	920	1004	3727	1016	3849	1070
351	10	718	88	921	1003	3731	1020	3865	2
352	9	721	925	937	268	3733	75	Ecru	387
353	6	722	323	943	188	3746	1030	B5200	1

* DMC Light Effects E168 can be substituted for regular DMC floss if preferred. There is no metallic colour match available in Anchor so please use 234 if converting.

About the Author

Emma Congdon studied Graphic Design at the University of the Arts London. She worked as a graphic designer for advertising and design agencies for many years before rediscovering her love of cross stitch and becoming a freelance designer in order to pursue this passion. Her design work regularly features in magazines such as *Cross Stitcher*, *Cross Stitch Crazy* and *World of Cross Stitching*, and she has designed several pieces for DMC. This is her third book, and follows the success of her first two publications, *Cross Stitch for the Soul* and *Cross Stitch for the Earth*.

Acknowledgements

Many thanks for all the hard work put in by everyone at David and Charles in the making of this book. In particular Ame Verso for commissioning the idea, as well as designer Sam Staddon for such beautiful layouts once again. Thanks to Jane Trollope, my editor, for all of her attention to detail, and ability to make sense of my waffle. To the stitchers involved in creating the models, Sharon Atkinson, Eleanor Cooper, Glenda Dickson, Sandra Doolan, Nicola Gravener, Michelle Luscombe and Kirsty Torrance, thank you so much, you've done a sterling job and I could not be prouder. Jason Jenkins, thank you for photographing them all so wonderfully too. Thank you to my family for your love and support as always, and a special shout out to my darling baby daughter Skye (who decided to arrive early and before the book deadline!).

Index

A DAVID AND CHARLES BOOK
© David and Charles, Ltd 2022

David and Charles is an imprint of David and Charles, Ltd
Suite A, Tourism House, Pynes Hill, Exeter, EX2 5WS

Text and Designs © Emma Congdon 2022
Layout and Photography © David and Charles, Ltd 2022

First published in the UK and USA in 2022

A catalogue record for this book is available from the British Library.

ISBN-13: 9781446309209 paperback
ISBN-13: 9781446381618 EPUB
ISBN-13: 9781446381601 PDF

This book has been printed on paper from approved suppliers
and made from pulp from sustainable sources.

Printed in the UK by Pureprint for:
David and Charles, Ltd
Suite A, Tourism House, Pynes Hill, Exeter, EX2 5WS

10 9 8 7 6 5 4 3 2 1

Publishing Director: Ame Verso
Senior Commissioning Editor: Sarah Callard
Managing Editor: Jeni Chown
Editor: Jessica Cropper
Project Editor: Jane Trollope
Head of Design: Anna Wade
Designer: Sam Staddon
Pre-press Designer: Ali Stark
Photography: Jason Jenkins
Production Manager: Beverley Richardson

David and Charles publishes high-quality books on a wide range of subjects.
For more information visit www.davidandcharles.com.

Layout of the digital edition of this book may vary depending on reader hardware and display settings.